W9-CHZ-185

SUSTAINING OUR ENVIRONMENT

# Energy

Jill Laidlaw

Published by Amicus
P.O. Box 1329, Mankato, Minnesota 56002



Printed in the United States of America at Corporate Graphics, in North Mankato, Minnesota.

Published by arrangement with the Watts Publishing Group Ltd., London.

Library of Congress Cataloging-in-Publication Data
Laidlaw, Jill A.
Energy / by Jill Laidlaw.
p. cm. -- (Sustaining our environment)
Includes index.
Summary: "Discusses the carbon footprint of energy and ways that the environmental impact of energy can be reduced"—Provided by the publisher.
ISBN 978-1-60753-136-4 (library binding)
1. Power resources--Juvenile literature. 2. Power resources--Environmental aspects--Juvenile literature. 3. Renewable energy sources--Juvenile literature. I. Title.
TD195.E49L33 2011
333.79--dc22

2009029985

Series editor: Adrian Cole
Art director: Jonathan Hair
Design: Simon Borrough
Picture research: Diana Morris

Acknowledgements:
Gregory Bergman/Alamy: 27. Yann Arthus-Bertrand/Corbis: 29. Andrew Chambers/ istockphoto: 8. W Cody/Corbis: 28. Francis Dean/Rex Features: 9b. Jack Dempsey/AP/PA Photos: 20. Jerry Driendl/Getty Images: 14-15b. Felipe Rodriguez Fernandez/Getty Images: 19. Warren Gretz/NREL: 24. Brenda Hayward/Christian Aid: 17. Geoffrey Holman/istockphoto: 31. Fred Hoogervorst/Panos: 18. Hufton & Crow/View: 40. iofoto/istockphoto: 13t. Alex Kuzovlev/Shutterstock: front cover. Benjamin Lazare/istockphoto: 26. Nature Air: 35. Jan Oelker/RE Power: 21. OpenHydro Tidal Technology: 23t. Pelamis Wave Power: 23b. Penfold/istockphoto: 32. Practical Action: 39l. Thomas Prichard/istockphoto: 14t. Geoff Renner/Rex Features: 25. Rex Features: 34, 37cl. Sipa Press/Rex Features: 13b. SmartHomeUSA.com: 37cr. Abbie Trayler-Smith/Panos: 38. Solar Cookers International: 38r. Jochen Tack/Alamy: 10. Ray Tang/Rex Features: 16. Tesla Motors: 41. Graeme Whittle/istockphoto: 9t.

1213
32010

9 8 7 6 5 4 3 2 1

# Contents

# What Is Energy?

We owe everything to the sun. It's where all our energy originates, from the energy in food to the energy stored in fossil fuels (coal, oil, and gas) that has been locked away for millions of years. We use energy to take care of ourselves at a basic level—for light, heat, and shelter—and we use yet more energy to create consumer goods, such as televisions, and to power cars and other forms of transportation. We can't make energy—we can only transfer it from one form to another.

"Electricity is the life-blood of civilization. Without it we spiral down into anarchy and chaos."

Ian Fells, Emeritus Professor and Energy Policy Analyst, University of Newcastle, 2008

▲ **A city lights up at night. Electricity is mostly generated using steam turbines powered by burning fossil fuels.**

## Beginnings

The invention of the steam engine in 1769 by James Watt, a Scottish engineer, allowed us to harness energy on an industrial scale for the first time. The steam engine drove the Industrial Revolution, which took place in Western countries before anywhere else. The Industrial Revolution was powered by fossil fuels. More than 200 years later, industrialized societies are still primarily powered by fossil fuels. Steam engines are still in use—they are even a part of nuclear power plants.

## Measuring Power

- Units of electrical power are called watts (W) and are named after James Watt.
- A kilowatt (kW) is 1,000 watts. Look at a lightbulb—it will have its power rating written on it as a number of watts. If a lightbulb is rated at 100 watts, then it uses 1 kW of power in 10 hours. Power companies charge customers per kilowatt-hour.
- A megawatt (MW) is 1 million watts. A gigawatt (GW) is 1 million kilowatts.

## Unsustainable, Nonrenewable Energy

One problem with fossil fuels is that they are dirty. Burning coal, oil, and gas, and using gasoline and diesel, produce a range of pollutants including sulfur dioxide, nitrogen oxide, and particulates, which can harm people's health. Although emissions can be limited using "clean-up" technology, such as catalytic converters, they have been linked to a range of environmental and health problems. Using fossil fuels also produces carbon dioxide ($CO_2$)—a "greenhouse gas" that is thought to be the main contributor to man-made global warming (see pages 14–15). Another problem with fossil fuels is that they are finite and nonrenewable—one day we will use them all up and we will be unable to replace them.

**▼ We rely heavily on fossil fuels in every part of our lives, such as gas-powered stoves in our homes. But gas is a nonrenewable source of energy.**

## Sustainable, Renewable Energy

While fossil fuels will be with us for many years to come, the race is now on to replace them with energy that is both clean and renewable. This book will look at some of the problems and some of the solutions in this quest for sustainable energy.

**▲ Greenpeace campaigners dump coal to highlight the problems that will be created by building more coal-fired power plants.**

"What is required is an industrial revolution for sustainability, starting now."

John Schellnhuber, Chief Scientific Adviser to Angela Merkel, German Chancellor, 2008

# Energy Usage and Reserves

Most people living in more developed countries have access to a wide range of energy sources. Electricity is supplied via a distribution system, such as a national grid, connecting every power station and substation in a country.

## Less Developed Access

In less developed countries, people living in cities usually have access to some form of supply grid, but supply can be unreliable and expensive. People in rural areas often have to meet their own energy needs, usually by collecting and burning wood.

**▼ National grids are monitored closely to maintain supplies.**

## Number Crunching

It's difficult to accurately measure how much energy people use—some countries don't keep complete records of their energy consumption. However, it is possible to estimate global energy use and to see trends. Between 1980 and 2005, worldwide energy consumption increased by 50 percent. About 86 percent of the energy we use comes from fossil fuels (mostly oil and coal). The vast majority of this energy is used by Western industrialized nations. The United States uses more energy than any other nation on Earth—25 percent—but only has 5 percent of the world's population.

**▼ This map shows direct oil usage per person in 2007.**

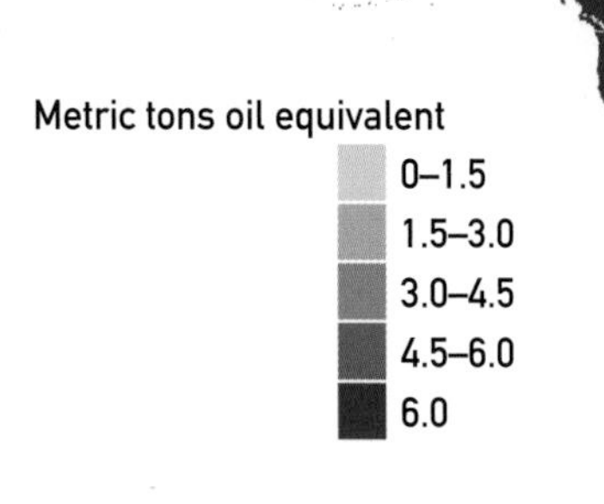

## New Economies

China and India both have rapidly growing economies, and their need for energy reflects this. The International Energy Agency believes that just two countries—China and India—will be responsible for 45 percent of the increase in world energy usage by 2030.

## Calculating Reserves

In 1914, the U.S. Bureau of Mines declared that there was only enough oil left for 10 years. In 1939, the U.S. Department of the Interior announced that there was only 13 years of oil left. Both estimates were wrong. How do we know how much energy we have left? It is difficult to answer this question accurately, as methods of calculation change, estimates of the size of fossil fuel deposits change, cars and industry become more efficient, and rates of consumption fluctuate.

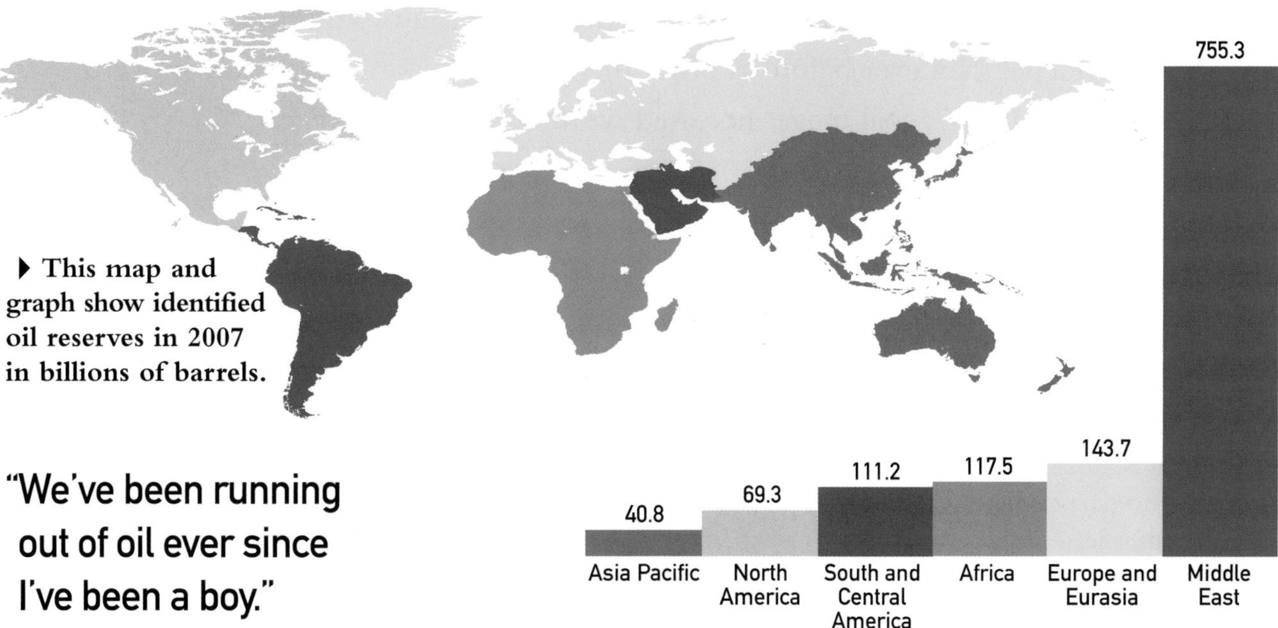


▸ **This map and graph show identified oil reserves in 2007 in billions of barrels.**

"We've been running out of oil ever since I've been a boy."

Professor Frank Notestein, Princeton University, 1994

## The Hubbert Peak

In 1956, M. King Hubbert, an American geophysicist, predicted that U.S. oil production would peak in 1970. The oil industry ignored Hubbert—until 1970, when U.S. oil production did peak. Since 1970, the United States has bought more and more oil from the Middle East. Hubbert also predicted that worldwide oil production would peak by 2010. The International Energy Agency currently estimates that the worldwide oil peak will be reached in 2020.

## Debate: Should We Worry about Energy Reserves?

No. Some scientists believe that

- the worldwide oil peak won't arrive for 20 to 30 years;
- there are untapped oil regions, such as polar areas, that will offset the peak;
- we have hundreds of years of coal left;
- industry is becoming more and more efficient, so fuel reserves will last longer.

Yes. Some scientists believe that

- we have overestimated world oil, gas, and coal reserves—the situation is worse than Hubbert suggested;
- extracting oil from the polar regions will be too expensive and have too great an impact on the environment to be allowed;
- demand from less developed countries is accelerating.

# The Consequences of Energy Use

The use of fossil fuels worldwide has environmental consequences, especially as demand continues to rise in the wake of economic growth in countries such as India and China. But it is not just these growing economies that are contributing to the jump in fossil fuel consumption. Russia, the United States, and some European countries are using more coal than ever before as other fuel sources become more expensive. Between 2004 and 2007, coal usage increased worldwide by 22 percent.

## At What Cost?

There are high environmental costs to our ever-increasing need for energy.

- Mining pollutes and is dangerous. Open-pit coal mining in particular scars the landscape, as does mountaintop mining, which literally takes the tops off mountains.
- Drilling and laying pipelines in wilderness areas, such as Alaska and Siberia, can damage wildlife and change the appearance of the countryside.
- The generation of electricity through coal-fired power plants releases a great deal of $CO_2$ into the air. Electricity generation via nuclear power has radioactive by-products that must be stored for many thousands of years.
- Cars are responsible for significant $CO_2$ emissions and other pollutants, which damage air quality, human health, and the environment.

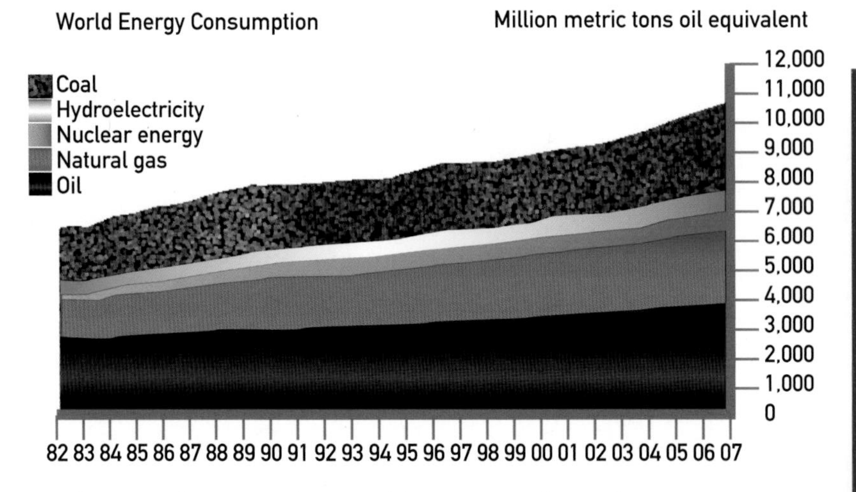


**▲ This graph shows the world consumption of energy from different sources from 1982 to 2007.**

### Debate: China's Dependence on Coal

- China uses coal to generate 70 percent of its energy needs.
- It is estimated that up to 20,000 miners in China die every year in accidents such as floods, cave-ins, and gas explosions.
- In 2007, China opened two new coal-fired power plants every week.
- Pollution from coal-fired power plants can cause lung diseases, cancer, skin conditions, acid rain, asthma, smog, and mercury contamination.

Some Western nations want to dictate energy policy to China. Why do you think they want to do this, and do they have the right?

▲ **Mining pollution leads to environmental damage.**

> "The EU wants different sources of supply [from Russia] . . . We must not sleepwalk into Europe's energy dependence crisis."
>
> José Manuel Barroso, President of the European Commission, 2008

### Campaign: Greenpeace Ban the Bulb

We can all make small changes to cut down energy use. Greenpeace is running a campaign called Ban the Bulb, calling on national governments to phase out traditional incandescent lightbulbs and legislate for the use of energy-efficient compact fluorescent lightbulbs. It is estimated that if everyone in the world switched to compact fluorescent bulbs, we would save enough energy to close 270 coal-fired power plants. In December 2007, the Irish government announced that it would ban incandescent bulbs starting in 2009. Australia, Canada, and the European Union (EU) are also phasing out incandescent bulbs.

▲ **Greenpeace spells out their campaign message with life preservers.**

## The Rise of "Energy Superpowers"

Many nations do not have enough energy to meet demand, so they import oil, coal, and gas from countries that have a surplus of these commodities. Saudi Arabia is the world's leading exporter of oil, followed by Iran. Both of these countries are members of OPEC (Organization of the Petroleum Exporting Countries). There are 12 OPEC countries, and they consult each other on how much crude oil to produce every year, as demand fluctuates. Russia also has large oil and gas reserves and, along with the OPEC countries, wields enormous power through the ability to withhold production of fuel and also to set world energy prices.

# Global Warming

Global warming is the name given to changes in the surface-air temperature of the Earth. The average temperature of our planet has gone up 1.4°F (0.8°C) since 1880. Many scientists think that this recent rise in temperature is due to an increase in the release of greenhouse gases, principally $CO_2$, into the atmosphere. $CO_2$ is produced when fossil fuels are burned, so many people believe that our use of fossil fuels is causing global warming. If burning fossil fuels is causing our planet to overheat, then we have to find alternative ways of supplying ourselves with energy.

"Melting glaciers will trigger mountain floods and lead to water shortages in South Asia and South America. Rising sea levels could inundate Small Island Developing States. Reduced rainfall will aggravate water and food insecurity in Africa."

Ban Ki-Moon, UN Secretary-General, talking about climate change, 2007

### The IPCC

The Intergovernmental Panel on Climate Change was set up in 1988 by the World Meteorological Organization (WMO) and the United Nations Environment Programme (UNEP). Governments all over the world consult the scientists of the IPCC for information and policy advice relating to climate change. A report issued by the IPCC in 2007 stated that it was "very likely" that human activity was causing global warming. The report was compiled by 2,500 scientists from 130 countries.

▲ **Kyoto, Japan, became the focus of world leaders' attention when it hosted the UN summit in 1997.**

## Debate: The Causes of Climate Change

A few scientists disagree over climate change, arguing that

- there isn't enough data to be sure of the reasons for global warming;
- global warming is real, but it's not caused by the activity of people, it's part of a natural cycle;
- the climate models used to predict future temperature changes due to global warming are flawed.

What do you think? Does it matter who is right?

## The Kyoto Protocol

In 1997, delegates from all over the world met in Kyoto, Japan, to try to find a way to curb greenhouse gases. The agreements that came out of this meeting were called the Kyoto Protocol. The main aim of Kyoto was to reduce greenhouse gas emissions by 5 percent compared with emissions in 1990. The protocol came into force on February 16, 2005, and the nations who signed on have from 2008 to 2012 to meet the reduction targets they agreed to. The most economically developed countries were asked to make the biggest cuts, but they have also been allowed to offset any increases in their pollution through carbon trading.

The United States, currently the world's biggest polluter, did not initially sign the protocol.

## Carbon Trading

Industry is being pushed by government legislation to reduce energy consumption, but many companies complain that they need time to improve the energy efficiency of their businesses.

In order to help businesses in the transition to greater energy efficiency, the EU created the Emissions Trading Scheme (ETS) in 2005. Under this program, companies have to monitor and report their $CO_2$ emissions. They are issued with permits that tell them how much carbon they can release. If they emit more carbon than allowed, they can buy unused allowances from other companies, from their national governments, or from other countries outside the EU.

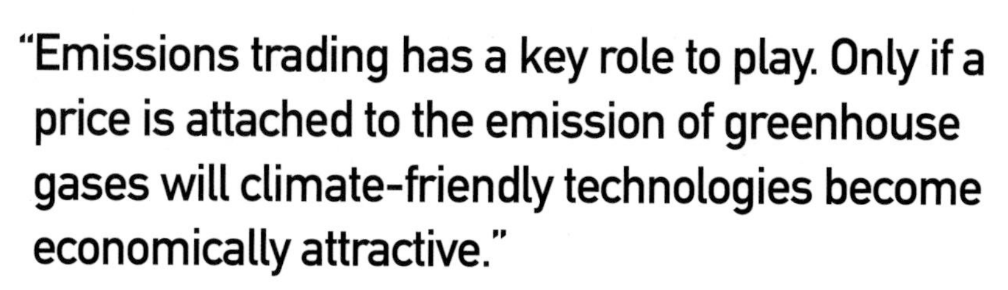

**"Emissions trading has a key role to play. Only if a price is attached to the emission of greenhouse gases will climate-friendly technologies become economically attractive."**

Angela Merkel, Chancellor of Germany, 2007

## Debate: Is Emissions Trading a Success or a Failure?

### It's a Failure

- Too many permits have been issued, so companies are still polluting—they're just paying more for it.
- It's unfair to companies who cleaned up before 2005.
- Permits should be auctioned—not given out for free—so that companies have to buy them and can't actually make money out of carbon trading.

### It's a Success

- Big power companies who have cleaned up their acts are still getting large permit allowances based on the emissions they used to release. They can trade their leftover allowances on the carbon market—now worth more than $50 million a year—which means that they can recoup some of the money they invested in energy efficiency and pollution cleanup. This is what ETS was meant to encourage.
- Carbon trading forces companies to account publicly for their emission levels.

## Campaign: Climate Camps

Camp for Climate Action began in 2006, when 600 people decided to gather in West Yorkshire at the site of the United Kingdom's most polluting power plants where they held 10 days of talks and workshops on sustainable living. In 2007, another climate camp protest was held next to Heathrow Airport to highlight people's objections to the building of a third runway. In 2008, eight camps took place around the world, and the movement is growing.

▼ This climate camp was set up next to Heathrow Aiport in 2007. People took part in peaceful demonstrations against airport expansion and the pollution additional air traffic would cause.

▲ Protesters gather as part of Christian Aid's Cut the Carbon campaign.

> "We can solve the climate change problem, but it needs concerted international efforts right now."
>
> Dr. Keith Allott, head of WWF-UK's climate change program, 2007

## The Energy Challenge

There are three major ways we can make our energy use more sustainable:

- improve renewable energy technology and increase its supply
- reduce the demand for energy
- achieve greater energy efficiency

## What Is Renewable Energy?

Renewable energy is energy that will not run out—it's energy we can always tap into because it will always be there. As long as the Earth's core does not go cold, as long as the sun keeps shining, as long as the wind blows, as long as the oceans exist, and as long as we produce plant and animal waste, we will be able to use geothermal, solar, wind, wave, and biomass energy sources.

## What Can Renewable Energy Achieve?

Renewable energy can

- help to reduce pollution,
- make fossil fuel resources last longer,
- give countries more energy security,
- give us more time to develop new forms of power.

> "I believe that the average guy in the street will give up a great deal, if he really understands the cost of not giving it up. In fact, we may find that, while we're drastically cutting our energy consumption, we're actually raising our standard of living."
>
> David R. Brower, American environmentalist, (1912–2000)

# The Power of the Sun

◀ Solar panels power this UN-led communication station in Mozambique.

The sun produces massive amounts of energy that finds its way to Earth as solar radiation, or solar energy. We can use this energy by simply designing buildings more efficiently—by making sure we have big windows that face the right direction and dark walls that absorb heat. We can also capture solar energy and use it directly or convert it into electricity using a number of different technologies.

## Solar Sources

- Passive solar energy is heat from the sun warming anything it falls on, such as swimming pools and buildings.

- Small-scale solar—an example of this technology is the small solar panels that can be fitted onto roofs that heat water running through them. These solar panels collect the heat of the sun and use it for a specific purpose.

- Solar power plants—mirrors focus the sun's rays to heat water into steam, which then drives a turbine to generate electricity.

- Photovoltaic (PV) panels use the sun's energy to generate electricity (see opposite).

"The use of solar energy has not been opened up because the oil industry does not own the sun."

Ralph Nader, American political activist

## Case Study: Field of Mirrors Seville, Spain

In March 2007, Europe's first commercial concentrating solar power plant using mirror arrays was opened just outside the city of Seville, Spain. A field of 600 massive mirrors moves to follow the progress of the sun throughout the day, reflecting its light and heat to focus on one point on a 40-story-high concrete tower. The tower uses this concentrated solar energy to heat water into steam, which is then forced into turbines that turn to generate electricity. The tower can power 6,000 households at the moment, but the plant is already being expanded with the addition of thousands of mirrors. The aim is to eventually supply electricity to the entire population of Seville, about 600,000 people.

## Debate:

Photovoltaic (PV) panels are solar panels fitted with PV cells made from silicon alloys that can change sunlight directly into electricity. PV cells are in widespread use—you can find them in watches and calculators.

PV systems
- are easy and quick to install
- can be manufactured in any size
- have a minimal impact on the environment and produce no $CO_2$ emissions
- domestically, can save an average household about $400 a year in electricity bills.

But:
- It would cost an average household anything between $12,000 and $35,600 to install PV panels.
- The performance of PV cells depends on the availability of daylight—most PV cells only provide about 10 percent efficiency.
- The metals that go into PV cells need to be mined, which can be damaging to the environment, and the manufacture of PV cells produces $CO_2$.
- PV cells are potentially toxic to dispose of.

If you could, would you invest in photovoltaic technology? Why?

▼ This is the solar tower of Seville's solar power plant. Each reflector measures about 1,300 square feet (120 sq m).

# The Power of Wind

The wind is an ancient source of energy. Windmills have been used for thousands of years to pump water, grind grain, and drive machinery. Modern windmills incorporate turbines that can generate electricity when powered by moving air. Wind power currently provides about 1 percent of the world's electricity.

## Wind Turbines

Modern wind turbines can be up to 20 stories high. Whatever their size, they typically have three blades that look like the propellers of an old-fashioned airplane. The blades are huge—some can have the same wingspan as a Boeing 747. When caught by the wind, the blades turn between 10 and 30 times a minute to drive a shaft inside the turbine connected to a generator, which converts this energy into electricity.

▲ **This is a wind turbine blade at the Vestas factory in Windsor, Colorado.**

"If the whole of Wales was covered with wind turbines, the nation would generate only a sixth of the UK's energy needs."

Professor David MacKay, physicist, Cambridge University, 2007

## Wind Farms

Large collections of wind turbines are called wind farms. Wind farms are usually built in places with strong and regular winds. These are often over large areas of elevated land unobstructed by windbreaks, such as trees.

### Debate:

What do you think about wind farms? Look at these points to start a debate:

### For Wind Farms

- a renewable form of energy
- electricity generation without emissions or waste products
- futuristic to look at—an inspiring symbol of green energy

### Against Wind Farms

- often uneconomic without huge setup subsidies from government
- unreliable, dependent on the wind
- ugly to look at, affects tourism
- noisy for people living nearby
- the electricity produced is relatively expensive
- can interfere with wildlife, particularly birds
- safety concerns—turbines can break apart, overheated machinery can catch fire

## Case Study: Wind Power in Germany

The German government has supported the growth of wind power by subsidizing the production and purchase of wind turbines and by guaranteeing the price at which people have to purchase wind-generated electricity. This means that wind power has expanded to provide 7 percent of German electricity needs. Around 20,000 wind turbines cover the landscape, more than 235,000 people are employed in the wind generation industry, and equipment sales topped $33 billion in 2007.

"Everyone wants wind power. If you ordered today [2008], you could possibly get a turbine in 2011 . . . It is a very good time for wind."

Spokesman for Enercon, a German wind system manufacturer, 2008

◀ This offshore wind farm is at Thornton Bank, Belgium. Each turbine produces 5 MW of power.

# The Power of Water

At the moment, the most widely used form of water energy is hydroelectricity. This uses the force of moving water to push the blades of a turbine, which in turn powers a generator to produce electricity. In the future, we may be able to take advantage of the marine energy technologies that are currently being developed. Although there are concerns about the impact of some of these technologies on the marine environment, they do not produce waste or $CO_2$ emissions and are renewable energy sources.

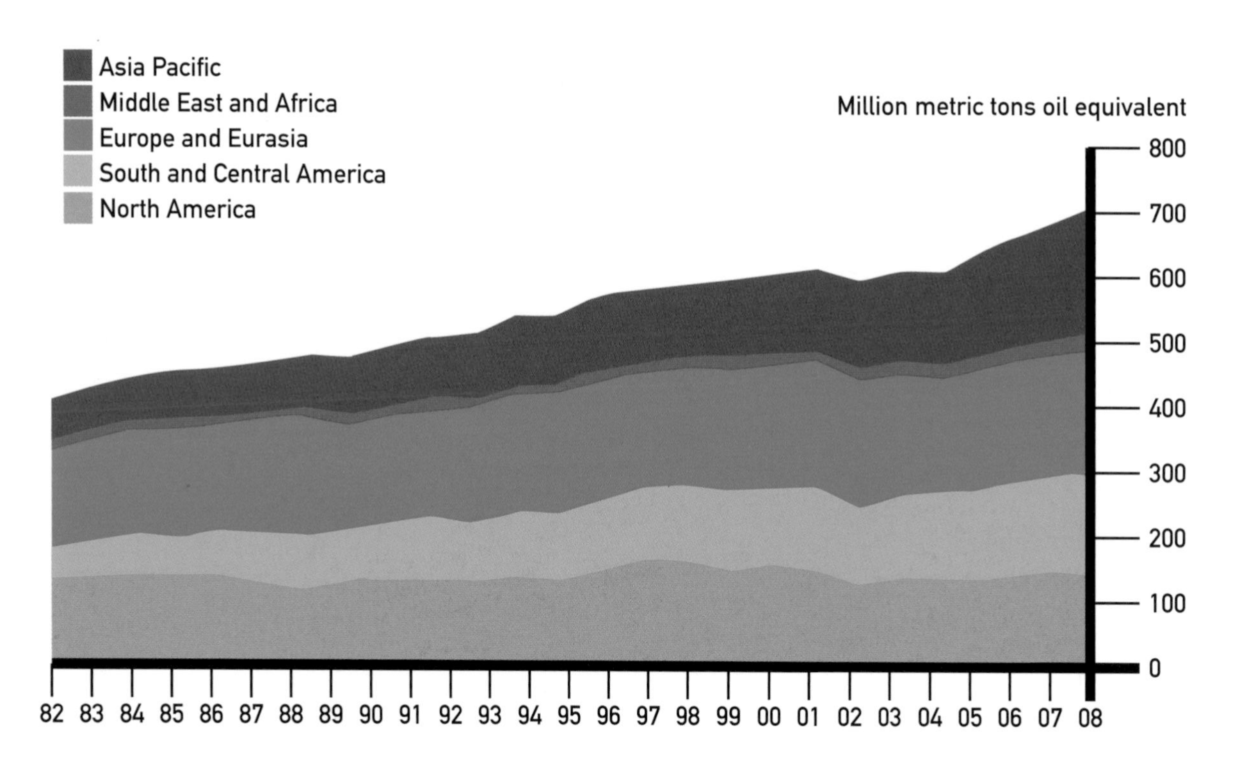


**▲ This graph shows the growth in global hydroelectric power generation from 1982 to 2008, measured in million metric tons of oil equivalent.**

## Tidal Barrages

Tides cause water levels at coastlines to go up and down, and we can take advantage of this movement. Barrages can be placed across inlets. Some work by capturing water when the tide rises. The trapped water is then emptied back into the sea through a turbine to generate electricity. Some barrages can produce electricity on both the incoming and outgoing tide. Some environmentalists are worried about the effects of barrages on wildlife and plants in estuaries. There are two large-scale tidal barrages operating in the world at the moment: in France, at La Rance, and in Canada, at Annapolis Royal, Nova Scotia.

## Tidal Turbines

Tidal turbines are like wind turbines but underwater, anchored to the seabed, converting the water that flows through them into electricity. Water is 800 times denser than air, so water turbines have to be very strong to withstand the water rushing through them.

▼ This raised tidal turbine was developed by OpenHydro.

"The sea is a harsh environment . . . the sheer force of fast-moving water is horrendous. It takes modern engineering capabilities to come up with solutions. Marine power subsidies are not as generous as they should be."

Peter Fraenkel, Technical Director, Marine Current Turbines, 2008

## Case Study: Wave Snakes in Portugal

In September 2008, the world's first commercial-scale wave-powered electricity generation plant was switched on at Aguçadoura, just off the northern coast of Portugal. From the shore, the power plant looks like a collection of long, thin red lines floating on top of the sea—these are wave snakes, and while they bob up and down, they convert the movement of the waves into electricity. There are three snakes at Aguçadoura, and they generate about 2.25 MW of electricity—enough to power more than 1,500 homes—but the Portuguese government is already planning to expand it and install another 25 snakes that will be able to create 21 MW of energy—enough to keep more than 135,000 households supplied with electricity.

▼ These wave snakes sitting off the coast of Portugal are 466 feet (142 m) in length and took 10 years to develop and construct. Each one is made of 772 tons (700 t) of carbon steel.

# Geothermal Energy

Geothermal energy is the name given to heat energy trapped under the Earth's surface. The Earth's core is as hot as the surface of the sun. By the time this heat has traveled to the 10 feet (3 m) of soil under our feet, it has dropped to a constant year-round temperature of between 50°F and 61°F (10°C and 16°C). The sun also heats the Earth's surface from above.

## Plug Directly into the Earth

Areas of fractured rock in the Earth's crust that are soaked in hot water or steam are called geothermal reservoirs. Wells can be drilled into these areas to allow the water and/or steam to come to the surface, where it can be converted by turbines into electricity, like a conventional power plant. The hot water can also be used to heat buildings.

## Pump Energy from the Soil

When the sun heats the Earth's surface, the heat can be extracted and used. Water-filled pipes are placed horizontally in trenches or vertically in wells, and the water is warmed by the surrounding heat in the ground. A heat pump can take this ground heat and use the energy to heat buildings in the winter and cool them in the summer.

"Geothermal power plants produce electricity about 90 percent of the time, compared to 65 to 75 percent for fossil-fuel power plants, and cause virtually no greenhouse gas emissions. Today, it is technically feasible to access enough geothermal power to meet all the world's energy demands."

Mike Crocker, spokesperson, Greenpeace USA, 2008

▼ These organic tomatoes have been grown hydroponically using geothermal wells to heat the greenhouse.

▲ All year round, tourists and locals bathe in the hot, mineral-rich water of the Blue Lagoon thermal spa baths, just outside of Reykjavik, Iceland.

## Case Study: Volcanoes and Hot Springs in Iceland

In the 1970s, Iceland was, like most developed countries, dependent on fossil fuels. But Iceland sits on the mid-Atlantic ridge, a fault line that graces the country with active volcanoes, glaciers, hot springs, and lava flows—all intense sources of geothermal energy. Iceland has invested in hydroelectricity, which now produces nearly 80 percent of its electricity, and in geothermal power plants, which supply almost 20 percent. Hot water is pumped from boreholes sunk to a depth of between 650 and 6,560 feet (200 and 2,000 m). Geothermal energy is used to power everything from aluminum smelting to the hydroponic growing of tomatoes. The government is researching the use of geothermal electricity to split hydrogen from water to make hydrogen fuel cells to run the country's fishing fleet, buses, and cars, which are currently running on fossil fuels.

Iceland's National Energy Authority has issued figures that claim that only 20 to 25 percent of the country's hydroelectric capability and 20 percent of its geothermal potential has been tapped—and that Iceland could supply the northern hemisphere with a huge amount of renewable energy in the years to come.

"Iceland is only a short distance away from becoming the first economy completely powered by renewable energy."

Geir Haarde, Prime Minister of Iceland, 2008

# Beautiful Biomass?

▲ **Cow-pie power! Special biomass plants can use animal waste to generate clean power.**

Biomass energy comes from any plant and animal material. Biomass includes everything from the heat from wood on an open fire to ethanol produced from corn.

### Carbon Neutral

As they grow, plants and trees take in $CO_2$. In other words, they store energy absorbed from the sun. This is called photosynthesis. The chemical energy in plants is passed on to animals when they eat the plants, and on to us when we eat the animals. When we burn biomass, such as wood chips, peanut shells, straw pellets, elephant grass, or willow, stored chemical energy is released to give us heat. No extra carbon dioxide is released into the atmosphere as long as we replace the biomass we burn by replanting. This means that biomass can be carbon neutral.

### Other Types of Biomass

We can use the energy in waste. Domestic waste, such as lawn clippings and leftover food, is a valuable source of biomass. This waste can be burned in power plants to make steam, which can then be used to generate electricity. Much agricultural and industrial waste can be utilized in the same way, and waste oil can be used to power cars.

### Biomass Landfill

Biomass can be dumped into landfill sites and allowed to rot. Methane gas is released during the rotting process and can be collected and used as an energy source. Farmers place the manure from their animals into huge tanks, called digesters, to collect methane on a domestic scale.

"Biomass plants can help us in the fight against climate change, but only if they make the most of the waste heat they produce and use fuel from carefully chosen sources. Otherwise they're cutting down trees, shipping them across the world, and then throwing away the energy they get from them."

Doug Parr, Chief Scientist, Greenpeace, 2008

## Case Study: Biofuels

Corn, sugar, potato skins, rice, and wheat can be fermented to produce ethanol, a fuel that can be used by itself (mixed with 15 percent gasoline) to drive specially adapted engines, or 10 percent ethanol can be added to 90 percent gasoline to reduce carbon monoxide emissions. Biodiesel, another type of biofuel, can be made from vegetable oil, fat, or grease, and diesel engines can run on it without any modifications.

## Debate: A Burning Issue and a Growing Problem?

### For

- Burning biomass still pollutes the air, but not to the same extent as fossil fuels.
- If more biomass and waste is burned, then less has to be buried in landfill sites.
- Methane is a greenhouse gas, so if it is collected from landfill sites, it does not reach the atmosphere.
- Biomass production can provide income for farmers.

### Against

- Methane gas collected from landfill sites has to be treated before it can be fed into natural gas pipelines, and this is expensive.
- There is a danger that valuable wildlife habitats are destroyed to provide land for biomass to be grown.
- Biomass production can use land that could be used to grow food, and this causes food prices to rise.
- Some biofuels need a lot of fertilizer and other inputs that need energy, usually oil, to produce them.

◀ The United States supplies about 3 percent of its energy through biomass, produced at plants like this one.

# Nuclear Energy

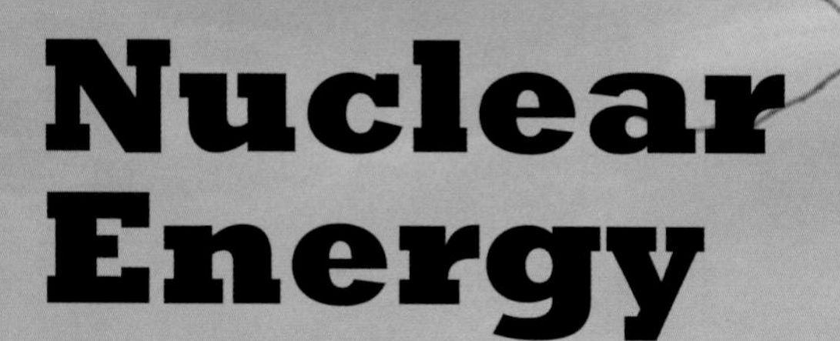

People often have strong opinions about nuclear energy. For decades, environmentalists have campaigned against nuclear energy because it produces waste that some scientists estimate will take 10,000 years to decay to a safe level of radioactivity. But in recent years, some green activists have started to support nuclear power because it is clean energy—it doesn't produce carbon dioxide, so it doesn't contribute to global warming.

**◀ These are nuclear plant cooling towers in Pennsylvania. The United States generates 20 percent of its electricity through nuclear energy.**

## Clean Energy from a Nonrenewable Source

Nuclear energy is not only a clean source of energy, but it can generate a huge amount of electricity—one ceramic uranium fuel pellet is about the size of your fingertip and contains as much energy as 150 gallons (570 L) of oil. Nuclear power plants pack these pellets into metal fuel rods, called fuel assemblies, which power the plant. The main ingredient of these fuel pellets is U-235, which is quite rare and needs to be extracted from uranium—the nonrenewable source. Uranium is highly radioactive and emits powerful energy. This can be harnessed, but high levels of radiation can cause serious damage to the environment and can kill plants, animals, and people.

## Case Study: Nuclear Energy in France

France doesn't have any oil or any gas and has very little coal. In the 1970s, the French relied on countries in the Middle East to supply them with oil for their oil-burning power plants. But in 1973, the price of oil increased fourfold, and the French were faced with fuel shortages and very high energy bills. The French were uncomfortable that they were so reliant on foreign imports to meet their energy needs, and they had very real concerns over long-term energy security. In 1974, the French government brought in a huge nuclear energy program and began investing heavily in new uranium processing plants and nuclear power plants.

Now nuclear energy supplies more than 75 percent of French electricity. French $CO_2$ emissions are the lowest in Europe, and electricity is France's fourth-largest export (prior to 1974, it was one of its biggest imports). But France has not resolved the issue of nuclear waste disposal, has experienced objections to underground burial throughout the country, and has no long-term plan in place to deal with waste.

▼ This is a reactor core inside a nuclear power plant.

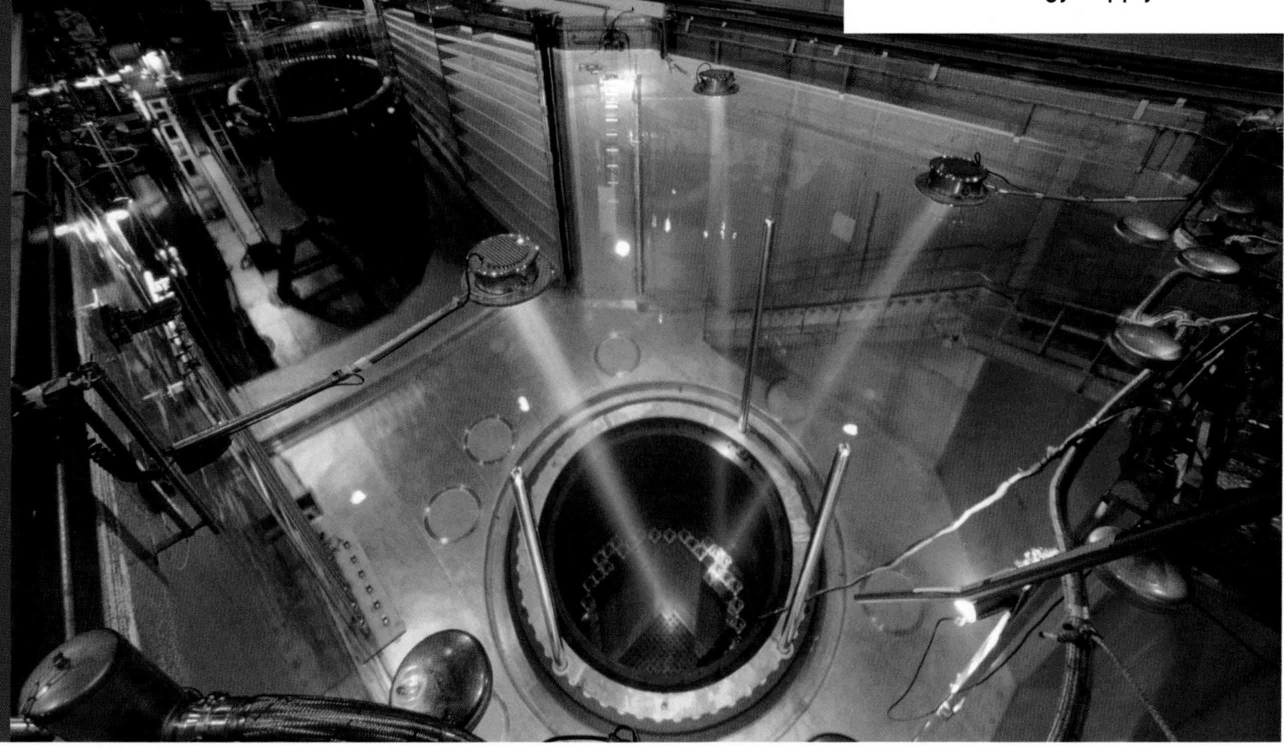

## Debate: Is Nuclear Energy the Way Forward?

Germany is committed to dismantling its nuclear power plants, and yet other countries, such as Italy, Malaysia, Nigeria, and Vietnam, have recently decided to start building nuclear infrastructures.

- At the moment, more than 15 percent of electricity worldwide comes from nuclear energy. Do you think this percentage should be higher?
- Are the problems of safe nuclear waste disposal outweighed by the advantages of a secure, clean energy supply?

**"In order to meet sustainable development goals, nuclear energy will have to achieve a higher level of social acceptance than it enjoys in many countries today."** Nuclear Energy Agency (NEA), France, reporting on nuclear energy and sustainable development

# Reducing Demand

Modern life would be unthinkable without electricity. But our electricity needs are steadily increasing. How can we meet this demand? We either have to generate more electricity, or we have to reduce the demand for electricity and use our existing capacity more efficiently. This second approach is called demand-side management (DSM).

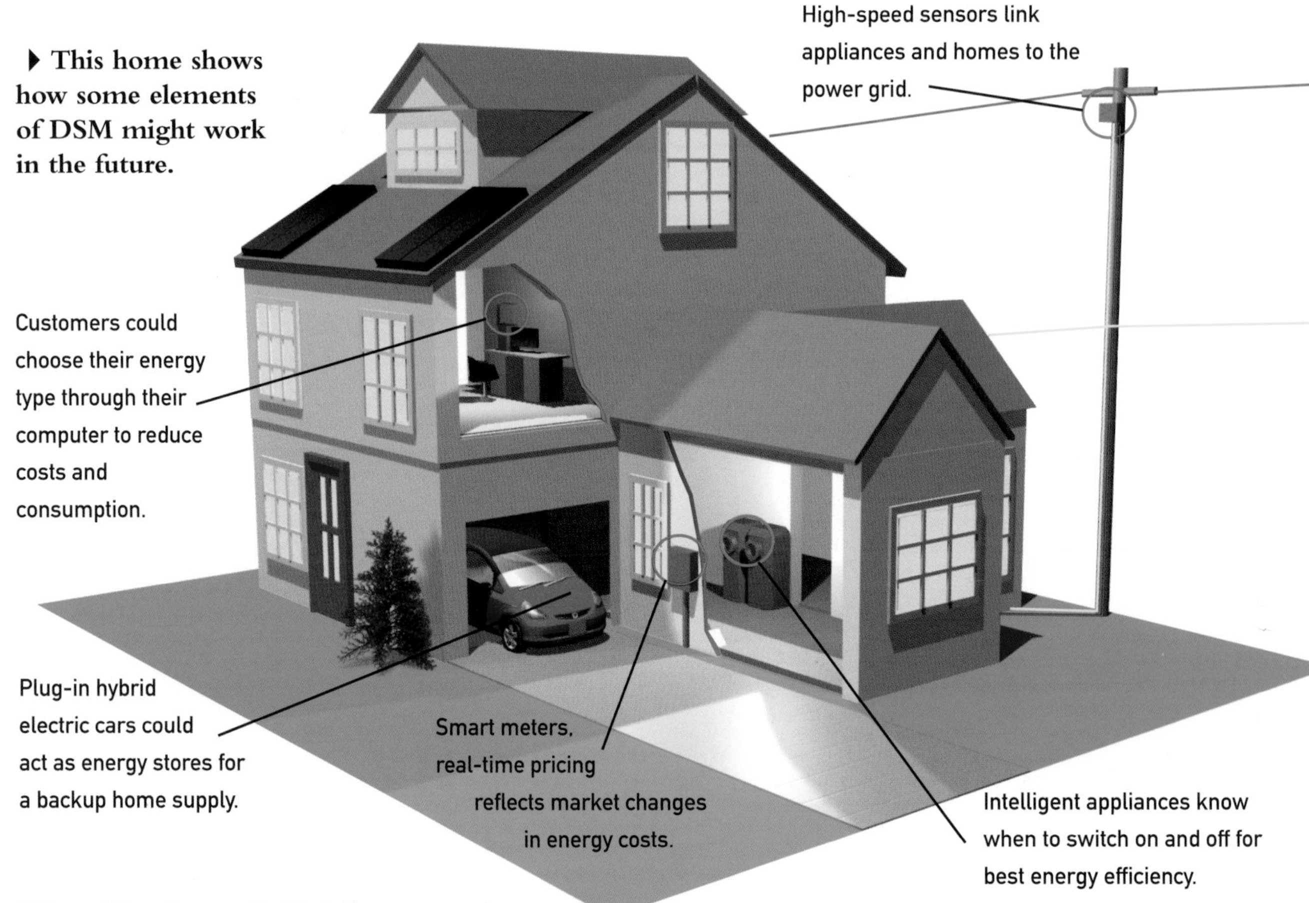


▸ **This home shows how some elements of DSM might work in the future.**

## The National Grid

In most developed countries, households access the electricity they need from the national grid. The national grid needs a minimum amount of power in order to remain stable. This is called the baseload demand. At the moment, baseload demand is maintained by power plants that are kept running all day, every day, fed by fossil fuels and nuclear power. To save energy, we can shift demand for electricity to off-peak times. This is called load management.

## Negawatts

Energy efficiency is the key idea behind demand-side management. Some energy companies work with their customers to reduce the amount of energy they use. Every watt of energy that is saved is called a negawatt. Energy companies rack up negawatts by, for example, sending energy-saving lightbulbs to their customers. This demand-side management saves them from having to make expensive changes to infrastructure, such as updating transformers.

### Case Study: Smart Fridges in the UK

In 2009, the British energy company NPower gave away 3,000 "dynamic demand" refrigerators (left), as part of a trial to reduce electricity demand in the United Kingdom. Dynamic demand technology consists of a small algorithm device, which is fixed inside the fridge and monitors the frequency of the national grid. When the frequency drops below 50Hz—for instance, when everybody makes a cup of tea in the commercial break of a popular TV soap opera—backup power plants supply the extra energy needed to keep the grid going. When surges of power are needed by the grid, the algorithm device reduces the amount of electricity the fridge uses but still maintains the temperature. Dynamic demand technology can be fitted into air conditioners, immersion heaters, and a range of other appliances.

"Dynamic demand [has] the potential to reduce greenhouse gas emissions and increase the grid's capacity to absorb wind energy—key elements of the government's energy strategy for renewables."

Lord Hunt, (UK) Minister for Energy and Innovation, 2008

"If you changed all your remaining bulbs to energy-saving ones, over the course of their lifetime, they will save you £600 [$973] and 2.7 tonnes [3 tons] of $CO_2$."

Philip Sellwood, Chief Executive of the Energy Saving Trust, 2008

### Campaign: The International Energy Agency (IEA)

Since 1993, the IEA (which is part of the Organisation for Economic Co-operation and Development) has sponsored a Demand-Side Management Programme that provides governments and energy companies with information and resources on DSM and energy efficiency. Eighteen countries, including Australia, the United States, the United Kingdom, France, India, and Japan, are working together to increase awareness of DSM around the world.

# Energy-Efficient Business and Industry

In the developed world, industry is trying to adapt to new energy efficiency standards and legislation, as nations try to meet their targets to reduce $CO_2$ emissions.

### Legislation

Most developed countries now have legislation relating to energy efficiency. Industry has to reduce its environmental impact by becoming resource efficient, investing in new technologies, and implementing environmental management.

▶ **Many offices now have energy-efficient equipment and lighting.**

"There are abundant opportunities to save 70 to 90 percent of the energy and cost for lighting, fan, and pump systems; 50 percent for electric motors; and 60 percent in areas such as heating, cooling, office equipment, and appliances."

Rocky Mountain Institute, Colo., on industrial energy efficiency

### Case Study: Energy Star

The Energy Star program, for energy-efficient products, is a labeling system that gives people information about the most energy-efficient models of appliances and office equipment. Equipment that carries the Energy Star label saves consumers money by being energy efficient. Office buildings can also earn an Energy Star rating for being energy efficient.

▶ This is the BP Shipping Environmental Management System (EMS). It is just one example of an EMS used to continually reduce and assess the environmental impact of a business.

PLAN
• Environmental aspects
• Legal requirements
• Objectives and targets: What do you want to achieve?

PERFORM 1
• Implementation and operation
• Staff training and awareness
• Communication
• Roles and responsibilities

PERFORM 2
• Measure, monitor, report, and track performance progress.
• Take corrective and preventative actions if necessary.

IMPROVE
• Management review: Were the goals achieved? What did you learn? Could things have been done better?

PLAN
PERFORM 1
PERFORM 2
IMPROVE

BP Environmental Charter

Compliance
Pollution prevention
Continual improvement

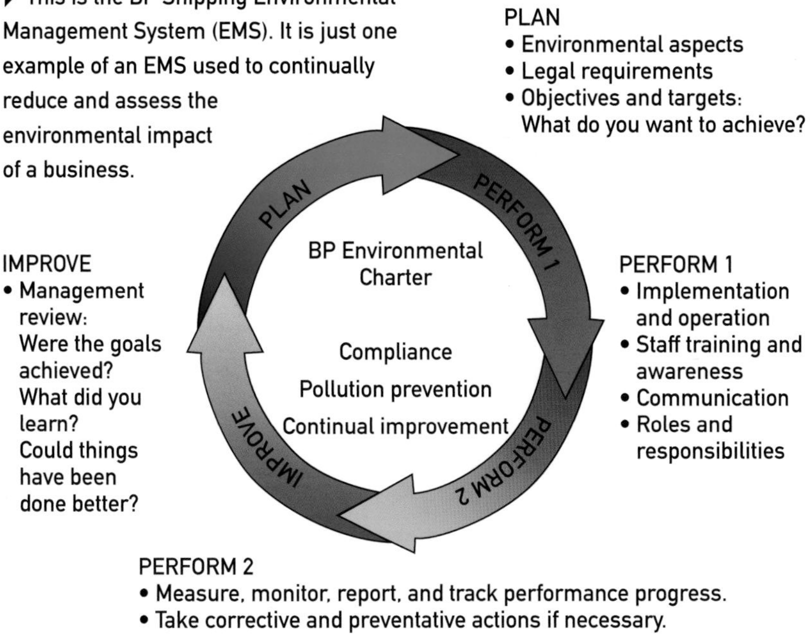

"Everyone agrees energy efficiency is a win-win situation . . . it reduces the environmental impacts of energy use, it's clearly the cheapest way to go, it makes money, and it has huge potential."

Bob Taylor, World Bank energy economist, 2008

## Environmental Mangement Systems (EMS)

Environmental management systems, such as the example above, are ways of setting guidelines within companies for environmentally aware behavior and practice. The environmental impact of a business/industry is assessed, and then an environmental policy is created that the company undertakes to enforce within an agreed time frame. Energy conservation is often a big part of an EMS system. Activities can include everything from switching off the lights to redesigning entire production systems.

## Ecodesign

Ecodesign incorporates energy efficiency into products before they hit the shelves. Ecodesign looks at the environmental impact of an item, such as a car or a kettle, over its whole lifetime. This is called "life cycle thinking." Manufacturers now have to consider the following before bringing a new product to the marketplace:

• Raw materials: Use as little as possible in the construction of the product, and try to reduce the distance the raw materials have to travel from the source to the factory and so save fuel.

• Packaging: Keep packaging design simple and materials to a minimum; make it biodegradable or recyclable.

• Making the product: Make the manufacturing process energy efficient, using renewable energy where possible.

• Use: If the product lasts longer, it will not need to be replaced as often and will have less environmental impact.

• Waste: Reduce dangerous waste and reuse waste within the company or within the manufacturing process.

• Transportation: Goods should be shipped as efficiently as possible; if the product/packaging is light, the truck transporting it will use less gasoline.

• End: The product should contain as little hazardous waste as possible so that disposal is safe. The product should be recyclable or have recyclable elements.

# Energy-Efficient Transportation

The environmentally friendly way to travel short distances is on foot or by bike. For longer distances, trains and buses are more energy-efficient options than cars. Even travel by car can be made more effective by carpooling—studies show that every car pooled takes between four and six cars off the road.

### Cars

More than 50 million cars are manufactured every year, and it is estimated that there are more than 700 million passenger cars in the world. In the eight most economically developed nations in the world (called the G8), there are about 750 cars for every 1,000 people, but in China, there are only 24 cars for every 1,000 people. It is predicted that China will become the world's second-largest market for cars in the world by 2010. One-third of global oil production is consumed by motor transportation every year.

▲ **Actor Kevin Bacon takes delivery of a Toyota Prius hybrid car.**

### Greener Cars

Forty years ago, cars were much less fuel efficient and more polluting than they are now. New greener transportation technologies are being developed all the time. These include hybrid and electric cars.

Hybrid cars use an electric battery in addition to a conventional internal combustion engine. When a hybrid car is stuck in traffic, the internal combustion engine switches off and the electric battery switches on. Hybrids travel farther on a tank of gasoline than conventional cars, so they emit less $CO_2$.

Electric cars use batteries that recharge by plugging them into the wall, so conventional fuel isn't needed at all. California and Hawaii, as well as Denmark and Israel, plan to build public charging sites to support a switch to electric cars.

"Environmentally friendly cars will soon cease to be an option . . . they will become a necessity."

Fujio Cho, President of Toyota Motors, 2004

### Case Study: A Carbon Neutral Airline in Costa Rica

NatureAir has seven small planes, like the one above, and flies 150,000 people across Costa Rica every year. NatureAir runs a carbon offsetting program—for every ton of carbon dioxide that it emits, it protects some rain forest by paying the owners of the land not to sell it to logging companies. About 0.7 square miles (2 sq km) has been saved since 2004.

"I think it's very important that aircraft manufacturers . . . share their views on the environment and the way for the industry to be more eco-efficient. We need to be united to win, because it's a battle for the development of air traffic."

Louis Gallois, Chief Executive of Airbus, 2007

### Debate: Should We Ban Flying?

Anti-airline campaigners say:

- High-speed rail links would provide more environmentally friendly transportation.
- Air transportation is the fastest-growing source of $CO_2$.
- Cheap air transportation just encourages unnecessary long-distance travel.

Airlines say:

- We are improving the energy efficiency of planes all the time, and by 2020 all new Airbus craft will produce 50 percent less $CO_2$ and 80 percent fewer nitrogen oxides than they did in 2000.
- Boeing's 777 Dreamliner airplane is 20 percent more efficient than average planes.
- Overall, planes produce fewer $CO_2$ emissions than cars or shipping.

# Energy Efficiency at Home

Heating, cooling, and lighting people's homes uses a lot of energy. It is thought that about a third of energy use in the United States is concentrated in people's homes and other buildings. In the United Kingdom, the government has set the ambitious goal of all new homes being energy efficient and zero-carbon-rated from 2016 onward. For a house to be rated as zero-carbon, it must be powered by renewable energy and not be responsible for any overall carbon emissions.

## Smart Energy Homes

Smart Energy homes (below) are due to be opened in Barcelona and Paris in 2009. These homes will use energy management systems that can turn heating and lighting on and off anywhere in the house by using sensors that detect whether people are in the room or not.

"The main goal with carbon neutral housing is to reduce carbon emissions and the risk of climate change."

Bill Dunster, architect of the BedZED ecovillage, 2008

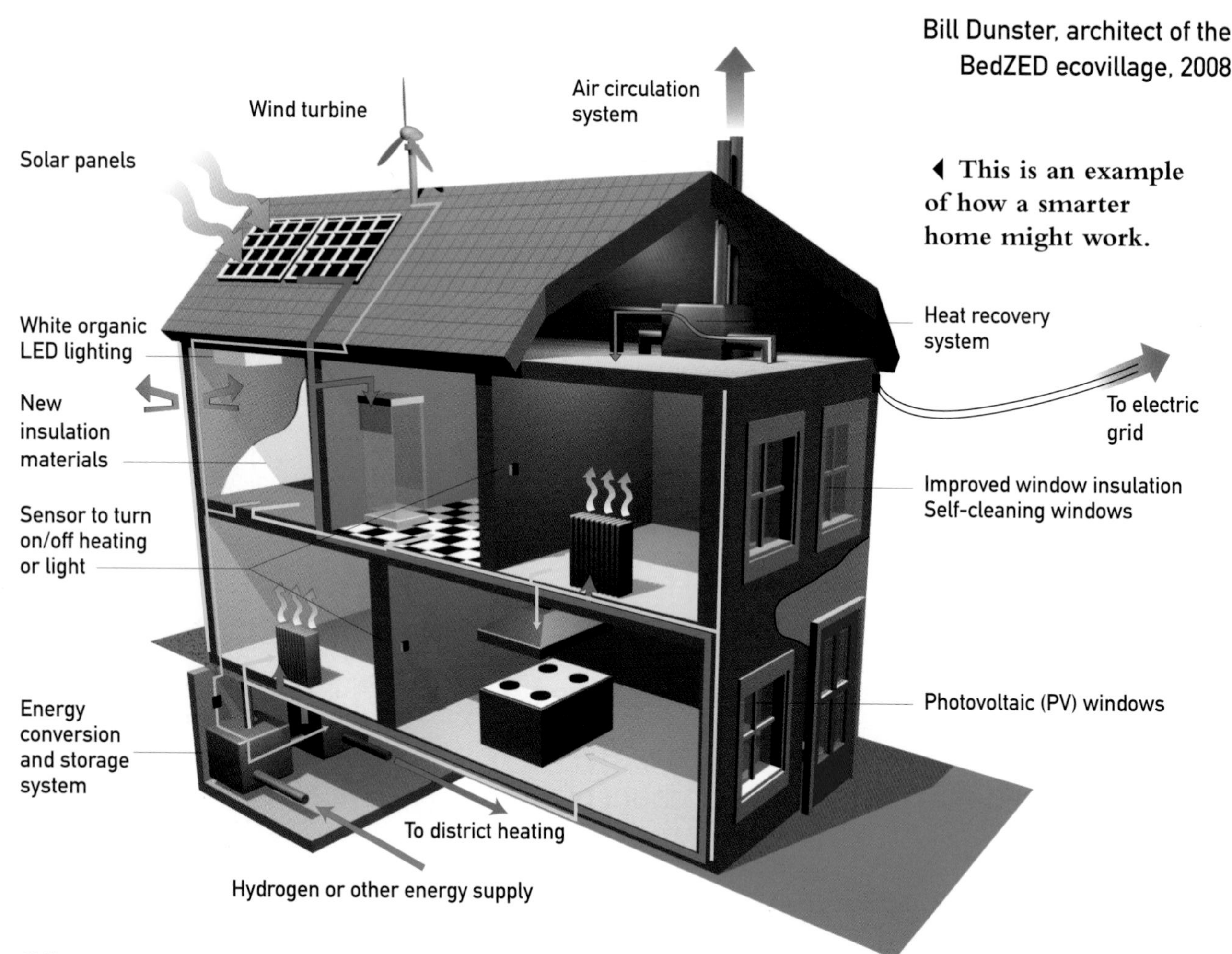


◀ This is an example of how a smarter home might work.

## Ways to Make Homes More Energy Efficient

- Sixty percent of heat loss is through walls, so insulate cavity walls.
- Unplug appliances when not in use because "standby" uses energy.
- Buy appliances that are ENERGY STAR qualified. They meet strict energy efficiency guidelines set by the government and can sae customers about a third on their energy bills.
- Install thermostats on radiators to reduce the heat in rooms that are not being used.
- Insulate the roof.
- Install smart meters—such as a PowerCost Monitor—so that the amount of energy being used can be clearly seen.
- Install energy-efficient lightbulbs —they use a fifth of the energy of traditional bulbs and last longer.
- Thirty-five percent of heat seeps out of closed windows, so weather-seal doors and windows.
- On hot days, turn on the air conditioner first thing in the morning and leave it operating at a lower rate for a longer time.

**▼ Devices such as the PowerCost Monitor, Kill A Watt EZ, and Smart Strip could save you money.**

**▼ BedZED is built on a small area of land in south London.**

## Case Study: BedZED

BedZED is a community of 82 ecohomes, workspaces, and gardens in Wallington, South London. BedZED is Britain's largest ecovillage. The homes in BedZED are very energy efficient—they use only 10 percent of the heating energy needed by conventional homes. All waste is composted or processed through a sewage treatment plant on site. The homeowners in BedZED recycle everything from food to shoes, and groceries are ordered in bulk to keep food miles and costs down. There's also a car club to encourage car sharing.

## Debate: Knock Down or Build?

- Constructing a new home creates about 55 tons (50 t) of $CO_2$.
- Refurbishing an existing home produces an average of 16.5 tons (15 t) of $CO_2$.
- It can take up to 50 years for a new home to "pay back" the extra expense of its energy-efficient features.

Should we build new homes or retrofit old ones to bring emissions down?

# Fuel Equity for All

Two billion people do not have access to electricity through a national grid. Sometimes this is because they live in war zones where power lines have been destroyed or in very remote areas where it's uneconomic to transmit energy. Some countries don't have a unified energy policy or an economy wealthy enough to invest in an energy infrastructure.

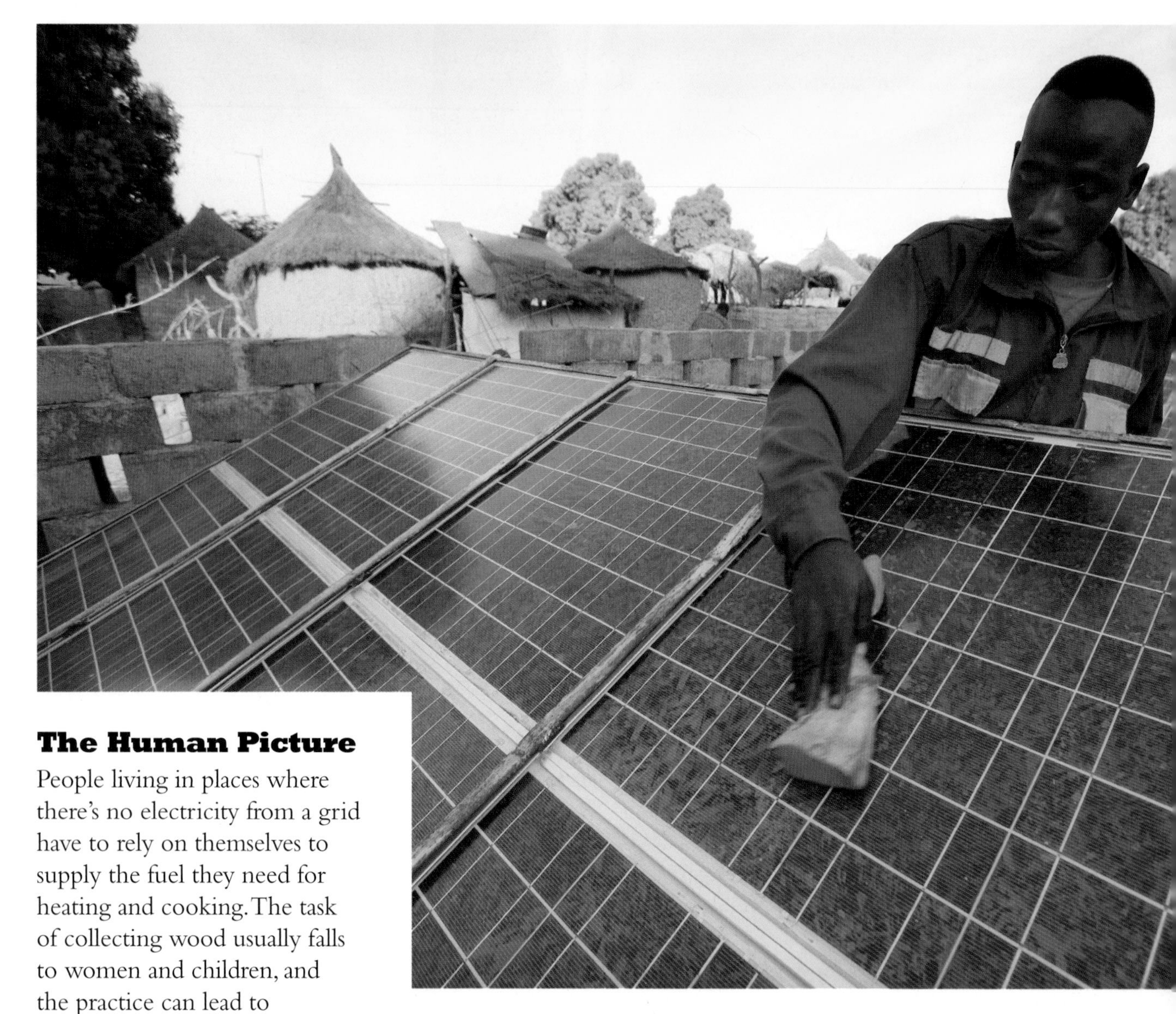

### The Human Picture

People living in places where there's no electricity from a grid have to rely on themselves to supply the fuel they need for heating and cooking. The task of collecting wood usually falls to women and children, and the practice can lead to deforestation, closely followed by poor crops delivered from degraded soil.

**▲ Cleaning solar panels in Tabakoro, Mali. These panels were installed as part of a Christian Aid program, and they supply power to the village water pump and electric lights.**

"It was wonderful! Straight away there was enough power to light a few lightbulbs, so I could work and the children could do their homework. I could charge up my own battery, and earn a little money by charging up those of my friends and neighbors, too."

Weerasinghe, subsistence farmer, Usgala Village, Sri Lanka, talking about his new wind turbine, 2008

## Case Study: Homemade Wind Turbines in Sri Lanka

In Sri Lanka, the Practical Action charity has been working to set up wind turbines, such as the one below, to provide electricity to isolated people and communities. There are 20 million people in Sri Lanka, and 20 percent of them—mostly in rural areas—are not connected to the national grid. Families without electricity sometimes spend up to 25 percent of their income on kerosene, and some have to travel for miles to buy it. Practical Action trains the villagers to install and maintain the wind turbines, and the turbine parts are made by locals from materials widely available in the area.

## Case Study: Solar Ovens

Solar ovens concentrate the sun's rays to cook food and are ideally suited to people living in hot countries. Simple CooKit ovens (above) are made of cardboard and aluminium foil and don't need any fuel—just the sun's heat. If people are given solar ovens, it frees up time from collecting wood, cuts down smoke-related health problems, such as asthma and eye infections, and ensures the safe preparation of drinking water.

# The Future

No one knows what our energy future will look like, but most people agree that it has to be clean and sustainable.

## Off-the-Grid Savings

While people in many areas of the world are struggling to get onto a national grid, some in the West think that the future of energy lies in getting households and communities off national grids and onto devolved grids. About 27 percent of energy generated in coal-fired power plants worldwide is "lost in transmission," so if electricity can be generated locally, huge savings could be made.

## Microgeneration

More and more people are taking responsibility for their own energy needs—from switching to energy-efficient lightbulbs to installing their own wind turbines. Innovations such as household-based heat pumps, solar panels, and biomass boilers can meet people's energy needs, and any excess electricity can be fed into a national grid system. This is called microgeneration. About 100,000 households in the United Kingdom use microgeneration, but 2 million houses in Germany already use these technologies.

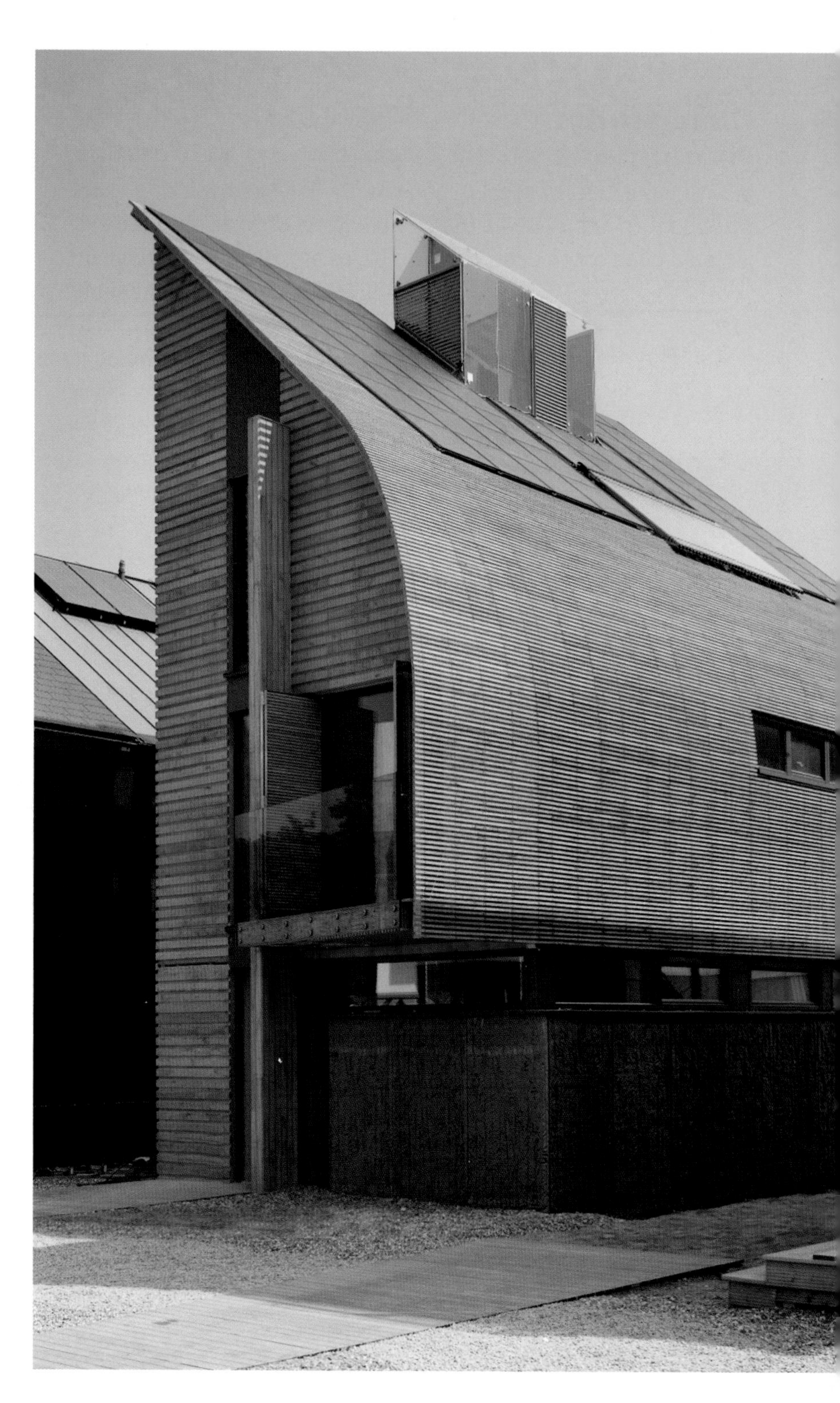

**▸ Increasingly, modern houses like this one are being built with microgeneration technology installed.**

"Microgeneration has the potential to make a significant contribution to overall energy use in the UK and, combined with energy efficiency measures, will help toward reducing our carbon emissions. The concerned individual can take an active role in the battle against climate change."

Malcolm Wicks, UK Minister for Energy, 2008

## Combined Heat and Power

Combined heat and power (CHP) plants are much more efficient than traditional power plants because they capture the heat that is the by-product of burning coal or gas and use it to heat and provide hot water for nearby communities. CHP is widely used in Scandinavia, Europe, and some parts of the United States, and more and more countries are beginning to build CHP plants to improve energy efficiency. Recent advances in technology have created a micro-CHP unit the same size as a domestic boiler that can be installed in people's homes—giving every family the potential to run their own mini power plant.

## Hydrogen—the Fuel of the Future?

Hydrogen is found everywhere in the universe. The sun and other stars contain hydrogen, as do water, biomass, coal, and gasoline. Hydrogen can be isolated by splitting water using electrolysis, and it can be used to generate both electricity and heat without any damaging emissions. Hydrogen batteries are called fuel cells. They can store energy for long periods of time and are activated by oxygen to generate electricity. The fuel cells can be used to power cars, computers, and mobile phones, and to provide emergency electricity for hospitals. Hydrogen technology is expensive at the moment, and we don't have the facilities to make it cheaply on a large scale, but investment is taking place around the world. In South Korea, for example, the government is giving huge subsidies to businesses that decide to install fuel cells in their office buildings.

"This [hydrogen fuel cell] technology is a must-have for the future of the Earth."

Takeo Fukui, president of Honda

**◀ Is this the car of the future? The Tesla electric sports car runs on the same kind of batteries found in laptop computers, but it can outrun a Ferrari Spider and is more fuel efficient than a Toyota Prius.**

# Glossary

**acid rain:** rain that contains harmful waste from burning fossil fuels

**asthma:** a breathing disorder that affects the lungs

**baseload demand:** the minimum amount of power that must be available at all times to service the needs of customers

**carbon dioxide ($CO_2$):** $CO_2$ is a gas found in our atmosphere that is vitally important to plants, used by them to make sugars during photosynthesis.

**carbon neutral:** having no net carbon emissions

**carbon offsetting:** paying to remove carbon dioxide from the atmosphere, such as planting trees to balance $CO_2$ emissions

**carbon trading:** countries and companies can trade metric tonnes of carbon dioxide internationally as a way of restricting $CO_2$ emissions.

**cavity walls:** exterior walls of a house that have a space, or cavity, between them

**demand-side management (DSM):** managing energy use by customers or populations to reduce demand on energy-generating plants

**dynamic demand:** technology that adjusts electricity consumption in response to the availability of power

**emissions trading programs:** programs that allow companies/countries to trade $CO_2$ emissions allowances

**hybrid cars:** cars that use combinations of two or more power sources, such as gasoline and electricity

**hydroponically:** when plants are grown in gravel and fed with nutrient-rich water

**Industrial Revolution:** in the late eighteenth and early nineteenth centuries, Britain's economy changed dramatically with the invention of the steam engine by James Watt (1736–1819). The steam engine led to the industrialization of British society, the expansion of trade and industry, and the export of manufacturing technologies. This was called the Industrial Revolution, and it spread to Europe, America, and beyond.

**kerosene:** a highly flammable liquid used to power jet engines as well as domestic portable lamps and stoves

**landfill:** a hole in the ground used to dump waste materials

**life cycle thinking:** designing an object or service with every aspect of its life cycle in mind—raw materials, reliability, recyclability, and disposal

**mercury contamination:** something that has been poisoned, such as the air or soil, with the heavy metal called mercury

**methane:** a greenhouse gas produced by decomposing waste and animals

**national grid:** the name given to all the power plants, substations, and power lines that interconnect to provide electricity for an area

**negawatt:** a watt of power that is saved due to energy efficiency

**photosynthesis:** the process in which green plants convert carbon dioxide and water into carbohydrates using energy from the sun

**photovoltaic (PV):** solar panels that convert sunlight into electricity

**turbine:** a machine driven by water or gas to generate electricity

**zero carbon:** as with carbon neutral, having no net carbon emissions

# Web Sites

BioRegional: Solutions for Sustainability
**www.bioregional.com**
The web site of BioRegional, the sustainability charity behind the BedZED ecovillage. Click on the BedZED link to see a short film about how the ecovillage works.

Camp for Climate Action
**www.climatecamp.org.uk**
The Climate Camp web site has information on alternatives to fossil fuels and the locations of climate camps around the world.

Commonwealth Scientific and Industrial Research Organisation (CSIRO)
**www.csiro.au**
This web site has information on everything from solar-powered cars to how to improve the environmental performance of buildings.

GreenCar.com
**www.greencar.com**
Lots of information on all the different types of green cars available, reviews of cars, and information on how to convert your car to greener technology.

IEA: DSM
**www.ieadsm.org**
Web site of the International Energy Agency's Demand-Side Management Programme. Demand-side management news, publications, and projects.

IPCC
**www.ipcc.ch**
The web site of the Intergovernmental Panel on Climate Change.

Practical Action
**www.practicalaction.org**
The web site of a charity that installs appropriate renewable technology to people without electricity.

Solar tower in Seville
**www.inhabitat.com/2007/05/21/sevilles-solar-power-tower/**
Inhabitat is a web log that tracks design and technology that works toward a sustainable future.

U.S. Department of Energy
**www.energy.gov/energytips.htm**
Information on choices you can make every day to save energy.

Wave Power
**www.guardian.co.uk/environment/2008/sep/24/**
renewable.wave.energy.portugal
Go to this page on the *Guardian* newspaper's web site to click onto a short film explaining how wave snakes work.

Please note: Every effort has been made by the publishers to ensure that these web sites contain no inappropriate or offensive material. However, because of the nature of the Internet, it is impossible to guarantee that the contents of these sites will not be altered. We strongly advise that Internet access is supervised by a responsible adult.

# Index